W9-DGV-358

SPORTING CHAMPIONSHIPS
Kentucky Derby

Blaine Wiseman

WEIGL PUBLISHERS INC.
"Creating Inspired Learning"
www.weigl.com

Published by Weigl Publishers Inc.
350 5th Avenue, 59th Floor
New York, NY 10118

Website: www.weigl.com

Library of Congress Cataloging-in-Publication Data available upon request.
Fax 1-866-44-WEIGL for the attention of the Publishing Records department.

ISBN 978-1-61690-121-9 (hard cover)
ISBN 978-1-61690-122-6 (soft cover)

3 9547 00350 8434

Printed in the United States of America in North Mankato, Minnesota
1 2 3 4 5 6 7 8 9 0 14 13 12 11 10

052010
WEP264000

Weigl acknowledges Getty Images as its primary image supplier for this title.

Project Coordinator
Heather C. Hudak

Design
Terry Paulhus

All of the Internet URLs given in the book were valid at the time of publication.
However, due to the dynamic nature of the Internet, some addresses may have
changed, or sites may have ceased to exist since publication. While the
author and publisher regret any inconvenience this may cause readers,
no responsibility for any such changes can be accepted by either the
author or the publisher.

Every reasonable effort has been made to trace ownership and to obtain
permission to reprint copyright material. The publishers would be pleased
to have any errors or omissions brought to their attention so that they may
be corrected in subsequent printings.

CONTENTS

7

26

15

What is the Kentucky Derby?

Held on the first Saturday of May every year since 1875, the Kentucky Derby is the world's best-known horse race. It is also called the "Run for the Roses" because of the beautiful garland of roses awarded to the winner.

Each year, 20 horses and their **jockeys** compete for the honor of becoming the Kentucky Derby champion. The horses gallop around the track, sending dirt into the air and fans into a frenzy. The event attracts about 150,000 spectators to Louisville, Kentucky every year. They come for the race and several other events and activities that take place around the derby.

The Kentucky Derby is known as "The Most Exciting Two Minutes in Sports."

Many fans place bets on the race, hoping they will win money. Deciding which horse to bet on can be a difficult choice. Some people spend the entire season leading up to the Kentucky Derby studying the horses. There are many aspects that racing fans look at when choosing their horse. Some horses run better on a muddy track. Others run faster from the outside of the track than from the inside.

Many people choose their horse based on its name or colors. Racing horses often have interesting names. For example, Big Brown and Mine That Bird are the names of two Kentucky Derby winners.

CHANGES THROUGHOUT THE YEARS	
Past	**Present**
Aristides was the first Kentucky Derby winner.	Today, a bronze statue of Aristides stands in the clubhouse gardens of Churchill Downs, where the Kentucky Derby is held.
In 1883, the race track was first called "Churchill Downs" in a Louisville newspaper.	The track was officially named Churchill Downs in 1937.
The founder of Churchill Downs raised $32,000 to build the track.	In 1984, a 10-year project to repair and renovate Churchill Downs was started. The entire renovation cost $40 million.

The Trophy

Since the 50th running of the Kentucky Derby, in 1924, a golden trophy has been awarded to the winner. The 22-inch (56.88-centimeter) tall trophy sits on a base made of jade and weighs 56 ounces (1.59 kilograms). The trophy, which is topped by a horse and rider, is decorated with 12 emeralds and 50 rubies, as well as an 18-karat gold horseshoe.

Kentucky Derby History

Horse racing has been a popular sport around the world since ancient times. Thousands of years ago, Romans raced horses and chariots. These sports were even part of ancient Greek Olympics between 700 and 400 BC.

By the 1100s, the British had started importing Arabian horses that were known for their speed. They created the **thoroughbred** breed of horses by **mating** three imported Arabian horses with many **mares**. Over hundreds of years, the British **bred** faster horses, which nobility used for racing in pairs. By the early 1700s, racecourses were built across England. People attended races to bet on the horses. In 1750, the Jockey Club was formed to create rules for the sport. It remains the governing body of English horse racing today. By 1814, special events were being held for the best racehorses. To take part in these events, horses had to meet certain qualifications.

Horse racing became a popular pastime in the United States as well as overseas. The first racecourse in the United States was built on Long Island, New York, in 1665. By the late 1800s, there were hundreds of racecourses across the nation. Kentucky was especially well-known for its high-quality racehorses. It was the ideal place for a major horse racing event.

Most thoroughbreds can trace their heritage to three male Arabian horses that were imported from Turkey to England in the 1600s and 1700s.

Colonel Meriwether Lewis Clark, Jr. of Kentucky traveled to England and France to learn about thoroughbred horse racing. Clark attended the 1872 Epsom Derby in England before traveling to France. There, the French Jockey Club had formed the Grand Prix de Paris, the top horse racing event in France. Clark decided to organize a top-notch horse racing event in the United States.

When Clark returned to Kentucky, he founded the Louisville Jockey Club. It was modeled after the French Jockey Club. The Louisville group began raising money to build a quality racetrack. The track became known as Churchill Downs, after Clark's relatives, John and Henry Churchill. The Churchills donated the land where the track was built.

On May 17, 1875, 10,000 race fans gathered at Churchill Downs to watch 15 thoroughbred horses race around the new track. It was a clear day with perfect track conditions. Aristides, a horse that was jockeyed by Oliver Lewis, trained by Ansel Williamson, and owned by H.P. McGrath, finished the race in 2:37:45 to win the very first Kentucky Derby.

When Aristides won, H.P. McGrath was presented with a check for $2,850. Today, the winning horse's owner leaves Louisville with a **purse** of more than $1.4 million.

The term "derby" comes from the Epsom Derby, which was named after the Earl of Derby.

My Old Kentucky Home

Beginning in 1921, a song called "My Old Kentucky Home," by Stephen Foster, was played as the horses came onto the race track. Playing this song has become a tradition at the Kentucky Derby. Fans sing along to the song while the horses take their starting positions.

Rules of the Race

The Kentucky Derby features 20 horses racing counter clockwise around the 1.25-mile (2.01-kilometer) track at Churchill Downs. The rules of the derby are fairly simple. The horse that runs the fastest from the starting gate to the finish line is the winner.

1 Jockeys

Jockeys ride the horses, urging them to run as fast as possible. Traditionally, jockeys have a very small physical build. The shorter and lighter the jockey, the more energy the horse will have for running. The jockey steers the horse around the track, navigating it through the field of other horses and looking for the clearest path to the finish line.

2 The Rules

The official rules of horse racing were written in England in 1750. These rules were used for the Epsom Derby, which the Kentucky Derby was designed after. As part of the rules, no jockey can touch another jockey or a horse other than his own, and no jockey can try to use his horse to intimidate other horses. Jockeys and horses must follow the rules, or they could be disqualified from the race.

3 Beginning the Race
Every horse must start at the same time. The horses begin the race by breaking through the gates that hold them at the starting line. Sometimes, a horse breaks through the gate before the race has officially started. The horse is reloaded into its gate, and the race is started again.

4 Interference
If a horse moves out of its **lane** and blocks another horse from passing, it can be disqualified for interference.

Timekeepers

In the early days of horse racing, people used stopwatches to record the time when the horses crossed the finish line. When the race started, a black flag was lowered at the starting line. This told the timekeepers to begin timing. The timekeepers stopped their watches when the first horse crossed the finish line. Today, the Kentucky Derby uses electronic timekeeping devices to assist timekeepers. These machines mark the exact time a horse crosses the finish line. The new system helps the timekeepers avoid errors.

The Race Track

When the first Kentucky Derby was run, the track was 1.5 miles (2.4 km) long. In 1896, the track was changed to its current length of 1.25 miles (2.01 km). The track is 80 feet (24.4 meters) wide all the way around. This allows the horses plenty of room to move around each other.

Horses race around the dirt, oval-shaped track, beginning in a straight section. Then, they turn a 180-degree corner. They race the final 1,234.5 feet (376.3 meters) down the **stretch** to the finish line.

The Churchill Downs track officially opened on May 17, 1875. Four races were scheduled that day.

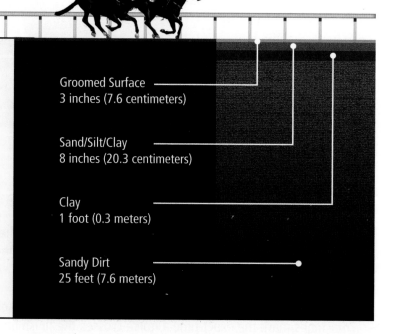

Under the Track

The Churchill Downs track was made with the safety of horses and riders in mind. Sandy dirt allows water to drain from the surface. On top of the sandy dirt sits clay, which makes a solid base for the track. The top surface of the track is a carefully mixed blend of sand, **silt**, and clay, making the track soft and safe. The surface is groomed to keep it extra soft so that the horses' hoofs are not injured by the solid base.

Groomed Surface
3 inches (7.6 centimeters)

Sand/Silt/Clay
8 inches (20.3 centimeters)

Clay
1 foot (0.3 meters)

Sandy Dirt
25 feet (7.6 meters)

The track is just one of the attractions at Churchill Downs. About 80,000 fans gather every year in the **infield** to watch the race, meet with friends, or picnic with family. Millionaires, actors, musicians, political leaders, and royalty watch the race from Millionaire's Row. This is an upscale seating area with dining facilities and a large balcony. Many people visit the Kentucky Derby Museum at Churchill Downs. Since opening in 1985, the museum has showcased the history of the event.

The Race Track

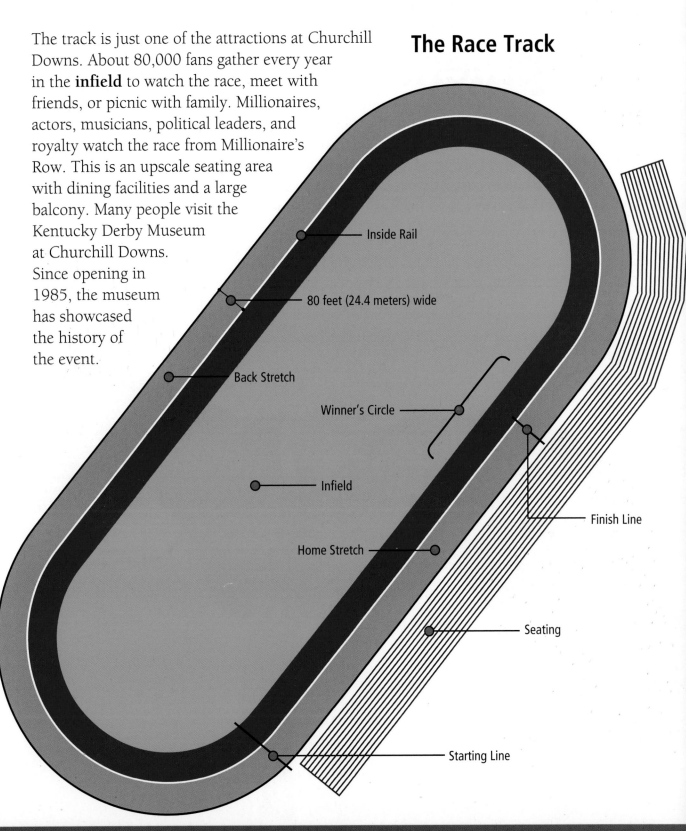

Inside Rail

80 feet (24.4 meters) wide

Back Stretch

Winner's Circle

Infield

Finish Line

Home Stretch

Seating

Starting Line

Horse Racing Equipment

T he most important pieces of equipment in horse racing are used to keep the horses and their jockeys safe from injury. Racehorses can be worth millions of dollars. Keeping these valuable athletes healthy is important. With horses competing in a tight, fast-paced race, accidents can happen. Protecting jockeys from injuries if they fall from their horse is a major concern.

A horse racing saddle is smaller than other types of saddles. Only 20 inches (51 cm) across the seat, a racing saddle sits near the horse's shoulders. During the race, jockeys do not sit in the saddle. They stand in the stirrups and crouch over the saddle.

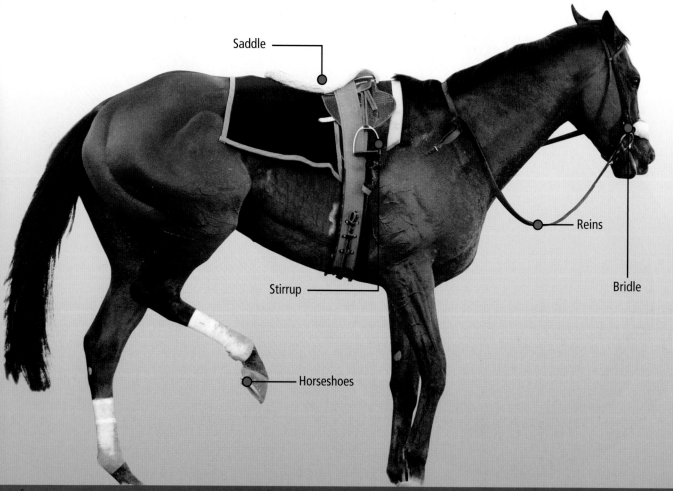

Saddle

Reins

Bridle

Stirrup

Horseshoes

Jockeys use reins to guide the horse around the track. The reins are attached to a bridle, which fits over the horse's head. By pulling the reins in a certain direction, the jockey turns the horse's head, making the horse run in that direction. By whipping the reins, the jockey tells the horse to run faster.

Racehorses wear different types of horseshoes, depending on the size of the horse, track conditions, and the trainer's preference. Aluminum shoes are lighter than steel shoes. However, steel is stronger, offering more protection to the horse's hoofs.

If a jockey falls off the horse during a race, it can be a very dangerous situation. With other horses following close behind and running at speeds of 40 miles (64.4 km) per hour, the jockey must be protected from stomping hoofs. All jockeys are required to wear helmets when racing and training. Helmets are made of lightweight, durable materials that protect jockeys from hitting their head on the ground and from the impact of a horse's hoofs.

Being trampled by a horse can cause serious injuries. Like a helmet, wearing a jockey vest can save a jockey's life. These lightweight vests protect major organs from being harmed if the jockey falls to the ground or is trampled by a horse. Jockey vests look like bulletproof vests and serve a similar purpose.

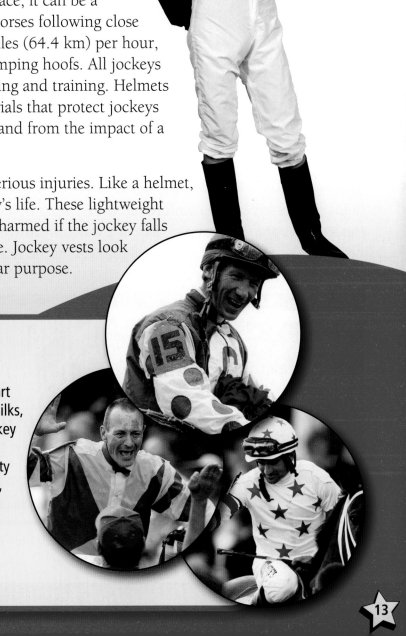

Helmet

Goggles

Silks

Silks

One way that people tell the horses apart as they race around the track is by the silks, or uniforms, the jockeys wear. Each jockey wears a different color and design. The body and sleeves can have a wide variety of patterns, including stripes, diamonds, stars, circles, or solid bands. Silks make the jockey and horse recognizable from all others in the field, helping race fans follow their favorite horse from start to finish.

Qualifying to Race

Qualifying for the Kentucky Derby is a once-in-a-lifetime opportunity. The race is only open to three-year-old thoroughbreds, so each horse only gets one chance to compete in the derby.

Most racehorses are born with the specific purpose of becoming strong athletes. This is because horse owners and trainers breed champion racehorses. They mate the fastest, strongest male and female horses to ensure the **foals** will have the features they need to be powerful racers.

Preparations for running in the Kentucky Derby begin when the horse is two years old. A horse trains for the derby by racing against the fastest horses in the world. This helps the horse become comfortable with

Grindstone won the Kentucky Derby in 1996. It was the second derby win for jockey Jerry Bailey.

the level of competition it will face at Churchill Downs. Only the best three-year-old horses are invited to run in the Kentucky Derby.

After all race fees have been paid, competing in the Run for the Roses can cost more than $200,000.

The Kentucky Derby is considered the jewel of the **Triple Crown**. This includes two other races for three-year-old horses, the Preakness Stakes and Belmont Stakes. It is the dream of all jockeys, trainers, and owners to take part in the derby. Owners pay large amounts of money just to **nominate** their horse for a chance to race in the three Triple Crown events. Owners who enter late must pay about $200,000 to be considered for a chance to run in these events. This money helps pay the cost of presenting the race and paying the winner.

Horses win a chance to compete in the derby by competing and finishing well in other races during the year. Only the top horses qualify, so horses that win or place in the top three at qualifying races during the year have a better chance of running in the derby. The horses that win the most money in the qualifying races are invited to race in the Kentucky Derby at Churchill Downs.

Owners hire veterinarians to look after their horse. Other owner expenses include trainer fees, jockey wages, and travel costs.

The Garland of Roses

In 1883, Colonel Clark saw a man presenting roses to all the women in attendance at a party after the race. This gave Clark the idea of making the rose the official flower of the derby. In 1896, the first bouquet of pink and white roses was presented to the winner, Ben Brush. In 1904, red roses were presented for the first time. Red continues to be the color used today. At the 58th Kentucky Derby in 1932, Burgoo King was presented with a garland of roses. A garland has been given to every winner since then.

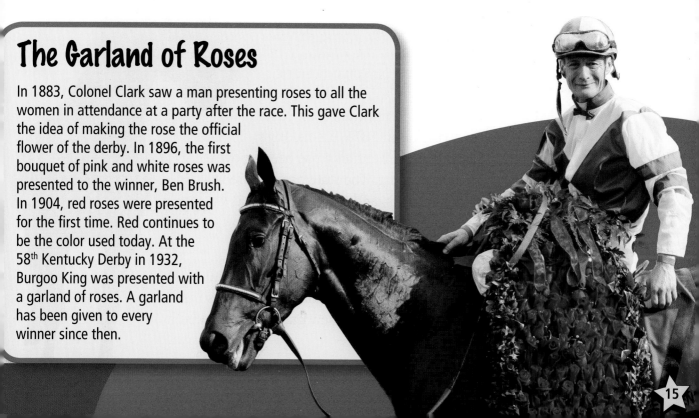

Where They Race

Kentucky has the most thoroughbred horse farms in the world. Most of the horses that win in Louisville come from Kentucky.

Churchill Downs is one of the best-known horse racing tracks in the world. In 1986, it was made a National Historic Landmark to honor its historical and cultural importance. Since its construction in 1875, the facility's home state of Kentucky has been known for horse racing. The state has hundreds of horse farms, and the thoroughbred is the state's official horse symbol.

The facilities at Churchill Downs have undergone several upgrades. Between fall 1894 and spring 1895, the track underwent its first major renovations. A new grandstand was built next to the track.

GET CONNECTED

To learn more about the Kentucky Derby, visit the official website at **www.kentuckyderby.com**.

The grandstand featured two spires on the roof that have since become a symbol of Churchill Downs and the Kentucky Derby. In 1960, a museum that focuses on the history of the derby and track was added. The latest upgrade was completed in 2005, after three years of construction at a cost of $121 million. During the upgrade, the clubhouse was replaced, 79 luxury suites were added, the twin spires were renewed, and new dining and entertainment areas were added.

Churchill Downs is the most-attended horse racing track in the United States. Though it has a seating capacity of 50,000 people, crowds can reach 150,000 on race day. People reserve seats up to a year in advance. After the horse race, the popular Kentucky Derby Parade is held. The competing horses and jockeys parade around the track to the cheers and salutes of the crowd.

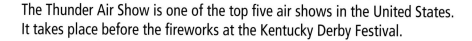

The Thunder Air Show is one of the top five air shows in the United States. It takes place before the fireworks at the Kentucky Derby Festival.

Kentucky Derby Winners from 2000 to 2009			
Year	Horse	Jockey	Time
2009	Mine That Bird	C. Borel	2:02.66
2008	Big Brown	K. Desormeaux	2:01.82
2007	Street Sense	C. Borel	2:02.17
2006	Barbaro	E. Prado	2:01.36
2005	Giacomo	M. Smith	2:02.75
2004	Smarty Jones	S. Elliott	2:04.06
2003	Funny Cide	J. Santos	2:01.19
2002	War Emblem	V. Espinoza	2:01.13
2001	Monarchos	J. Chavez	1:59.97
2000	Fusaichi Pegasus	K. Desormeaux	2:01.12

Mapping Horse Races of the World

ARCTIC OCEAN

NORTH AMERICA

PACIFIC OCEAN

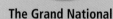TORONTO

ATLANTIC OCEAN

The Grand National
- Aintree, England
- Purse of about $1.35 million
- About 70,000 spectators

Queen's Plate
- Toronto, Canada
- Purse of about $1 million
- About 18,000 spectators

SOUTH AMERICA

Palio di Siena
- Siena, Italy
- No prize money
- About 60,000 spectators

SOUTHERN OCEAN

Legend

- Continents
- Oceans
- Cities

621 Miles

0   1,000 Kilometers

N
W ● E
S

ARCTIC
OCEAN

Prix de l'Arc de Triomphe
- Paris, France
- Purse of $5.85 million
- About 50,000 spectators

Japan Cup
- Tokyo, Japan
- Purse of about $6 million
- About 100,000 spectators

ASIA

AINTREE

EUROPE

PARIS

SIENA

Dubai World Cup
- Dubai, United Arab Emirates
- Purse of about $10,000,000
- About 30,000 spectators

TOKYO

PACIFIC
OCEAN

DUBAI

AFRICA

INDIAN
OCEAN

AUSTRALIA

DURBAN

Durban July
- Durban, South Africa
- Purse of about $400,000
- About 30,000 spectators

MELBOURNE

Melbourne Cup
- Melbourne, Australia
- Purse of about $5.5 million
- About 120,000 spectators

19

Women and Horse Racing

Traditionally, jockeys and racehorse owners have been men. However, there have been many influential women involved with the Run for the Roses.

In 1904, Elwood became the first horse owned by a woman to race in the Kentucky Derby. Laska Durnell and her husband, Charles, who was also the horse's trainer, both owned Elwood. Laska nominated Elwood for the Derby without telling Charles because he thought that the horse did not have the skill to compete at such a high level. Elwood won the race. He was the first horse owned by a woman to hold this honor. In addition, Elwood was the first derby winner that was bred by a woman, Mrs. J.B. Prather.

Rosa Hoots was also pioneer in Kentucky Derby history. In 1909, Rosa's husband, Al, bought a mare named U-See-it. Eleven years later, Al fell ill. Before his death, Al asked his wife to keep U-See-it and to breed the horse with a male horse named Black Toney. He believed their foal would one day run in the Kentucky Derby.

Jockey Rosemary Homeister has won more than 2,000 races. In 2003, she became the fifth woman to race in the Kentucky Derby.

GET CONNECTED

Learn more about the role of women in the Kentucky Derby at **www.kentuckyderby.com/ history/women-in-the-derby**.

Black Gold was born to U-See-it and Black Toney in 1921. Three years later, he raced in the Kentucky Derby, winning the event.

At the 1942 Kentucky Derby, seven of the top eight finishers were owned by women. This opened the door for women to become involved in other roles at the Kentucky Derby. In total, 13 women have trained horses that have competed in the derby. There have been a total of five female jockeys in Kentucky Derby history. The first was Diane Crump, who rode Fathom to a 15th place finish in 1970.

Diane Crump won more than 230 races in her career as a jockey.

Fantastic Fillies

Female horses have played an important role in the Kentucky Derby. Ascension was the first **filly** to run in the derby, finishing 10th at the first derby in 1875. Through the years, three fillies have won the derby. Regret won in 1915, Genuine Risk took the title in 1980, and Winning Colors was first to reach the finish line in 1988.

Historical Highlights

People who bet on Mine that Bird to win in 2009 earned the second-highest winnings in Kentucky Derby history. A person who placed a $2 bet received $103.20 in winnings.

Every year, the Kentucky Derby offers racing fans and participants many exciting moments. There is always a horse that is favored to win the derby, and there are also horses that are considered long shots to win. Sometimes, a horse runs at record-setting speed, breaking ahead of the group. Other times, several horses cross the line so close together that judges have to consult a photo.

The most unexpected long shot to win the Kentucky Derby was Donerail, who won in 1913. The **odds** on Donerail were 91.45 to 1. This meant that for every $1 a person wagered on Donerail, he or she was paid $91.45 when the horse won. The less likely a horse is to win the race, the higher the odds. People who bet on a horse with high odds will likely lose. If the horse wins, however, they earn much more money than if they had bet on a horse that was expected to win.

In 2005, race fans were treated to a battle between two long shots as Giacomo edged out Closing Argument for the garland of roses. The odds on Giacomo were 50.3 to 1, while Closing Argument's odds were 72 to 1.

In 1973, Kentucky Derby history was made when one chestnut thoroughbred dazzled Churchill Downs with a track record. In his most recent race before the derby, Secretariat finished in third place, which made many people doubt his speed and power. At the 99th Kentucky Derby, he blazed around the track in an incredible 1:59.4, becoming the first horse to run the Kentucky Derby in less than two minutes.

Monarchos is the second horse to win the race in under two minutes, winning the 2001 Kentucky Derby in 1:59.97. In 1973, Secretariat became the first horse to finish the race in under two minutes.

The First Five Kentucky Derby Winners			
Year	**Horse**	**Jockey**	**Time**
1875	Aristides	O. Lewis	2:37.75
1876	Vagrant	R. Swim	2:38.25
1877	Baden Baden	W. Walker	2:38.00
1878	Day Star	J. Carter	2:37.25
1879	Lord Murphy	C. Shauer	2:37.00

LEGENDS
and Current Stars

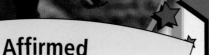

Big Brown

Affirmed

Affirmed

The 1978 Kentucky Derby featured one of the greatest rivalries in horse racing history when Affirmed and Alydar competed against each other. Alydar was considered the favorite to win. Early in the race, Affirmed fell behind Alydar but ran fast around the final turn. As Affirmed outran the pack, Alydar made a final push down the stretch. Affirmed beat Alydar to the finish, but only by a short **length**. The rivalry continued in the final two races of the Triple Crown. Affirmed narrowly outran Alydar by a neck at the Preakness and by only a head at the Belmont. No horse since Affirmed has won all three races in the U.S. Triple Crown. Alydar is remembered as the first horse to finish in second place in all three races of the U.S. Triple Crown.

Big Brown

Big Brown was named for his owner's business partnership with United Parcel Service (UPS). He was undefeated and the favorite to win the 2008 Kentucky Derby. Big Brown's jockey was Kent Desormeaux, who had won the Kentucky Derby in 1998 with Real Quiet and in 2000 with Fusaichi Pegasus. Desormeaux said that Big Brown was the best horse he had ever ridden. When Big Brown started in the 20th gate, the odds turned against him. No horse had ever won the derby starting from that gate. Big Brown stayed to the outside around the first turn, waiting for his chance to move up. Big Brown moved through the field of 19 other horses. In the end, only one other horse was close to the finish as Big Brown carried Desormeaux across the line. He was 4.75 lengths in front. Big Brown would go on to win the Preakness two weeks later.

Secretariat

Secretariat became a household name in 1973, when he broke the Churchill Downs track record. Secretariat raced around the track at a blistering pace, going head-to-head with his rival, Sham. Coming from the outside, Secretariat took the lead along the final stretch and won by 2.5 lengths, becoming the first horse to finish the Kentucky Derby in less than two minutes. He would further prove himself that same year by winning the Preakness and the Belmont Stakes to complete the U.S. Triple Crown.

Mine That Bird

Mine That Bird was not expected to win the 2009 Kentucky Derby, even though winning was in his blood. His father was Birdstone, who won the 2004 Belmont Stakes. His grandfather, Grindstone, won the 1996 Kentucky Derby, and his great-grandfather, Unbridled, won the derby in 1990. Despite his championship **pedigree** and his standing as Canadian champion, Mine That Bird entered the 135th derby as a long shot to win. He looked to be out early as he fell far behind the rest of the horses and spent most of the race in last place. As the pack rounded the final turn, Mine That Bird, ridden by jockey Calvin Borel, made a sprint to the finish. He passed every other horse along the way to win by 6.75 lengths. Only two weeks after his second Kentucky Derby victory, Borel and his **filly**, Rachel Alexandra, beat Mine That Bird at the Preakness by only one length. Borel rode Mine That Bird again in the Belmont Stakes, finishing third.

Secretariat

Mine That Bird

Famous Firsts

Aristides won the first Kentucky Derby, but he was not favored to win. In fact, even his owner, H.P. McGrath, did not expect him to win. McGrath owned another horse, Chesapeake, who he believed was faster than Aristides. He entered both horses in the race, hoping that Aristides would lead the way as a **pace horse**. When the time was right, McGrath thought Chesapeake would hit his top stride and take over the lead. As the two horses rounded the final turn, jockey Oliver Lewis saw McGrath signalling him to speed up for the win. Chesapeake's speed was fading, while Aristides appeared to be getting stronger. Aristides won the race for McGrath, while Chesapeake finished eighth.

A statue of Aristides was unveiled at Churchill Downs in 1987.

In 2009, 16.3 million viewers watched the Kentucky Derby on television.

African Americans have played a major role in the derby. Oliver Lewis, the first jockey to win the Kentucky Derby, was African American. In fact, 13 of the 15 jockeys who rode in the 1875 Derby were African American. Aristides, Lewis' horse, was also trained by an African American, Ansel Williamson. There have been several African American owners who have seen their horses race in the Kentucky Derby, but only one has won. In 1891, Dudley Allen's horse, Kingman, won the Derby in a time of 2:52 ¼. Allen also trained Kingman.

Until 1952, the only way to see the Kentucky Derby was to travel to Louisville. That year, the derby was broadcast nationally for the first time. This brought the Run for the Roses to a new audience. Today, the Kentucky Derby is broadcast globally to millions of viewers.

In 2004, a court decision allowed jockeys and horse owners to make money through advertising. For the first time, jockeys were allowed to wear corporate logos on their silks.

Prize Money

There is a large amount of money involved in the Kentucky Derby. The first time the purse was more than $100,000 was in 1954, when Determine won the race in 2:03. In 2004, the purse was one million dollars. In 2005, the purse was doubled to two million dollars.

The Rise of the Derby

1874

Colonel Meriwether Lewis Clark forms the Louisville Jockey Club.

1875

Aristides wins the first Kentucky Derby on a 1.5-mile (2.4-km) track.

1896

The track length is changed to 1.25 miles (2.01 km).

1909

Several states make horse racing illegal. Kentucky resists, allowing the derby to continue.

1913–1915

Kentucky Derby history is made three years in a row. In 1913, Donerail becomes the biggest upset winner in history. Old Rosebud sets a new track record in 1914, and in 1915, Regret is the first filly to win. These three accomplishments draw new attention to the derby.

1925

The derby is broadcast on network radio for the first time.

1935

The first Kentucky Derby Festival is held.

1945

The U.S. government bans all horse racing in March. The decision is changed in May, allowing the Kentucky Derby to be run for the 71st consecutive year.

1949

The derby is broadcast locally on television for the first time.

1968

For the first time, a Kentucky Derby racer is disqualified. Tests show that the horse Dancer's Image was given illegal medication. Forward Pass, who finished second, is declared the winner.

1973

Secretariat breaks the two-minute mark.

1974

A record crowd of 163,628 watches as Cannonade wins the 100th Kentucky Derby.

1999

The Kentucky Derby trophy is changed because of superstition. The horseshoe is turned to point upward so the luck will not run out.

2000

Marlon St. Julien becomes the first African American jockey to ride in the derby since 1921.

2004

Smarty Jones is featured on the cover of Sports Illustrated. It is the first time a derby winner is featured on the cover in more than 20 years.

QUICK FACTS

- The favorite dish served at the Kentucky Derby is Burgoo. This stew is made of lamb and vegetables.

- Twenty-nine horses have won the Kentucky Derby from the second post position. This is more than any other starting position.

Test Your Knowledge

1 What is the name of the horse and jockey team that won the first Kentucky Derby in 1875?

2 Where does the Kentucky Derby take place?

3 Who was the first filly to win the Kentucky Derby?

4 Who founded the Kentucky Derby?

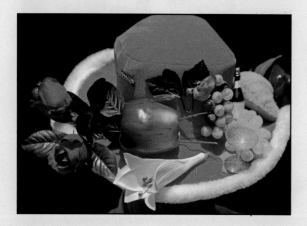

8 How old are the horses in the Kentucky Derby?

9 Which horse won the 2009 Kentucky Derby?

5 Which Kentucky Derby winner was the third horse to run the race in under two minutes?

6 Which Kentucky Derby winner was the least likely horse to win?

7 What two winning horses have finished the Kentucky Derby in less than two minutes?

10 In 2010, what anniversary did the Kentucky Derby celebrate?

ANSWERS: 1) Aristides and Oliver Lewis 2) Churchill Downs in Louisville, Kentucky 3) Regret 4) Colonel Meriwether Lewis Clark 5) Monarchos 6) Donerail in 1913 7) Secretariat and Monarchos 8) Three years old 9) Mine That Bird 10) 135th

Further Research

There is more information about the Kentucky Derby and horse racing available on websites and in books. To learn more about the Kentucky Derby, visit your library, or search online.

Books to Read

Search your library for books about the Kentucky Derby. On your library's computer, type in a keyword. The computer will help find information you are looking for. You can also ask a librarian for help.

Online Sites

Learn about the history of Churchill Downs at www.churchilldowns.com

To learn more about a certain horse, type the horse's name into a search engine, such as Google. Some horses have their own websites. Learn more about the fastest horse in history at www.secretariat.com

Learn all about the history of horse racing before the Kentucky Derby by visiting www.equine-world.co.uk/horse_sports/horse_racing_history.htm

Glossary

bred: mated a male and female horse

filly: a female horse less than four years old

foals: newborn horses

infield: the area inside the track

jockeys: athletes who ride horses in races

lane: a straight line of the track that a horse occupies while it is running, like a road lane

length: a racing measurement; the length of a horse is one length

mares: mature, female horses

mating: bringing two animals together to produce young

nominate: to propose or enter a horse as a possible Kentucky Derby contender

odds: chances of winning

pace horse: a horse that sets a consistent speed

pedigree: the record of a horse's ancestors

purse: the amount of prize money available to be won

silt: very fine sand, clay, or dirt

stretch: a continuous area of land

thoroughbred: a type of horse that is bred for racing

Triple Crown: a title given to those who win all three of the major horse races in a given country

Index